FRIENDS
OF ACPL

D1201929

LET'S GO TEAM:
Cheer, Dance, March

LET'S GO TEAM:
Cheer, Dance, March

Techniques of Dance for CHEERLEADING

Craig Peters

Mason Crest Publishers
Philadelphia

For Alexandra, to whose technique I would simply add: Dance like nobody's watching, sing like nobody's listening, and love like you'll never get hurt.

Mason Crest Publishers, Inc.
370 Reed Road
Broomall, PA 19008
(866) MCP-BOOK (toll free)
www.masoncrest.com

First printing

1 2 3 4 5 6 7 8 9 10

Library of Congress Cataloging-in-Publication Data

Peters, Craig, 1958-
  Techniques of dance for cheerleading / Craig Peters.
     v. cm. — (Let's go team — cheer, dance, march)
Includes index.
Contents: Dancing, cheering: what's the difference? — It's all about attitude — Stretching — Choreography — The three f's.
  ISBN 1–59084–531–5
1. Cheerleading—Juvenile literature. 2. Dance—Juvenile literature.
[1. Cheerleading. 2. Dance.] I. Title. II. Series.
  LB3635 .P44 2003
  791.6′4 — dc21
                           2002015952

Produced by
Choptank Syndicate and Chestnut Productions
226 South Washington Street
Easton, Maryland 21601

Project Editors Norman Macht and Mary Hull
Design Lisa Hochstein
Picture Research Mary Hull

Printed and bound in the Hashemite Kingdom of Jordan

OPPOSITE TITLE PAGE

Facial expression, body movement, and vocal ability are all important for cheerleaders to master if they want to succeed in competition.

Table of Contents

Dancing or Cheering?

You wake up in the morning after a good night's sleep with a few butterflies in your stomach. It's nothing too bad, actually. It feels more like excitement than fear.

After all, it's not like you're lacking in self-confidence or anything. You know the routine from start to finish, so that's not any problem. You can do this with your eyes closed. You're very excited for today's competition. Your energy is up, and your enthusiasm and anticipation are sky-high. You hope that everyone else you've been working with for months is just as psyched.

You've been practicing for weeks, refining your moves. At first you felt funny practicing in front of a

Dancing and cheerleading both require a high level of fitness, lots of practice, a positive attitude, and teamwork.

The mental techniques used by dancers can also help cheer-leaders to focus on their routines and show emotion in their performances.

mirror so much. After a while, the self-consciousness disappeared, and you were able to concentrate on making sure your arms and legs were in the right positions. You worked for what seemed like a hundred hours on keeping your head up, and on making sure your facial expressions were just the way you wanted them to be.

You have a good breakfast, but you don't eat anything too heavy. You want to feel good for today's competition.

You take time putting on your outfit. You want everything to be just right. The judges don't look for the tiniest imperfections, of course, but you notice them, and that's what counts right now. You want to make sure that everything is as perfect with your appearance as you know it will be in your performance.

When you get to the high school where the competition is being held, the butterflies come back a little bit as you see the parking lot packed with cars. The sidewalks are filled with families headed into the school together. The auditorium is going to be standing room only. The excitement and anticipation start building again deep inside of you.

You get inside the school and see everyone else in your group all clustered together, talking with excitement in their voices. You join the group and spend a few minutes reviewing some of the hardest moves in your routine. To make things perfectly synchronized at the right moment takes a lot of effort, and you all want to be able to smooth over those trouble spots you've been having during the last few practices.

The time for your group to take the stage is about a half hour away, so you find an open area backstage and spend some time stretching. You spend extra time stretching your legs. The last thing in the world you want is a cramp in your hamstring in front of the judges.

Now your time to take the stage is just a few minutes away. Everyone starts reminding each other of all the things to remember. Be sure to smile, but don't have a forced smile. Be sure to keep your arms like this at this part of the routine, and like that at the other part. Don't forget your position on stage with respect to the other people. Keep your back straight. Don't forget about keeping your head up and maintaining eye contact with the judges at the appropriate times.

This is it. The group before you passes by on their way to the dressing room area, the lights remain dark, and you take your position on the stage. Everyone else takes their positions all around you. Even though it's dark, you can still see the audience out there. Not their faces specifically, but their shapes and shadows. You know they're out there and that every seat in the auditorium is filled. The murmur of the crowd sends a small chill of excitement up your spine. In a moment, the lights will go on, and every one of them will be looking at you. You're as ready as you'll ever be.

The lights go on. There is some enthusiastic applause. You smile, take notice of the judges' table at the front of the auditorium, and stand still in preparation for your routine. You hear someone (your mom? your sister?) call out your name. Then a hush falls over the audience. Anticipation hangs heavily in the air as the music begins. Is it cheerleading music or dance music?

It could be either one. Because the scene above is repeated countless times each year at dance and cheerleading competitions around the world.

There are many similarities between cheerleading and dance. Both are very physical activities. Both require a

Unlike dancers, cheerleaders sometimes have a vocal component to their routines. It's one more thing cheerleaders have to perfect.

high level of fitness. Both require the participants to engage in a lot of training and practice. Both require positive attitudes.

Fitness, training, and attitude is what this book is about. On the pages that follow, you'll see how there are similarities between cheerleading and dance. Most important, you'll see how many of the physical and mental techniques used by dancers can also be used to help a cheerleader reach her maximum potential.

If you're a dancer who is thinking about taking up cheerleading, you'll see that the similarities between the

DANCE vs. CHEERLEADING: THE BIGGEST DIFFERENCE

Dancing and cheerleading have many similarities, but they also have one very big difference. It may seem obvious, but dancers (usually) don't have to worry about any kind of vocalizing during their routines.

At a dance recital, you're not likely to see a group of dancers on stage singing along to the music, much less chanting or cheering to the crowd.

For cheerleaders, it's one more piece of the performance puzzle. Cheers have to be learned, the voice has to be taken care of, and proper projection and breathing needs to be worked on. This all has to happen in addition to the physical moves of the cheerleading routine.

It may seem like a small thing, but it's not. In a very real way, cheerleaders are combining many of the elements of dance with many of the elements of singing. It's a difficult combination to master.

two will help you in your cheering. If you're a cheerleader who has been a dancer, you'll see how many of the things you learned in dancing classes carry over into the cheerleading world. And if you're a cheerleader who has never danced, get ready to pick up some new tips and techniques to help you be the very best you can be.

It's All About Attitude

Whether you're dancing or cheerleading, attitude counts. Take two dancers or cheerleaders with exactly the same physical skills. One has a positive attitude, and one has a negative attitude. Which one do you think will go further?

Dancers work hard on developing a positive attitude toward themselves, their bodies, and dancing as an art form. Martha Graham, the world-famous dancer and choreographer, said, "Nobody cares if you can't dance well. Just get up and dance. Great dancers are not great because of their technique, they are great because of their passion."

Cheerleading combines vocal elements with dance moves and gymnastic skills. A good cheerleader can put it all together into one convincing package.

Having and showing a positive attitude goes a long way toward improving your performance as a cheerleader or dancer.

That's a good quote for cheerleaders to remember, particularly while starting out. Cheerleading is a complicated mix of vocal and physical skills. Cheerleading includes elements of not only dance, but also gymnastics, singing, and acting. Cheerleaders have to be able to do all the right moves in just the right ways. They have to cheer while they're doing them, and they have to have the proper stage presence while moving their bodies.

If that all sounds like a lot to remember, well, it is. So you have to work on developing your mental skills in addition to your physical and vocal skills. That means developing and maintaining a positive attitude toward yourself and toward cheerleading in general.

As you work on learning the various skills that make a good cheerleader, remember Martha Graham's quote.

THINKING POSITIVE

One of the most popular books ever published on the subject of having a positive attitude is Dr. Norman Vincent Peale's *The Power of Positive Thinking.* Dr. Peale believed that the keys to happiness and success are all in your mind. By freeing yourself from self-doubt, he wrote, you can overcome any obstacle. In contrast, if you think negatively, it can actually prevent you from accomplishing your goals. Dr. Peale's book has been translated into more than a dozen languages and has sold millions of copies. One of its key messages can be summed up by the first two sentences of the book: "Believe in yourself! Have faith in your abilities!"

Easier said than done, for some people. If you're interested in exploring the subject further, there are countless books about how to develop and maintain a positive attitude. You may want to talk to parents, friends, and teachers about some of the best books they recommend, or check with your coach or local librarian.

There are also many quotations that serve as excellent reminders about thinking positive and maintaining a positive attitude. Baseball's legendary home run king Babe Ruth said, "Never let the fear of striking out get in your way." Walt Disney said, "If you can dream it, you can do it." Theodore Roosevelt said, "Your attitude about who you are and what you have is a very little thing that makes a very big difference."

Don't fall into the trap of thinking that such statements are corny. They're not. In fact, they're the keys to the kind of personal growth and success that you're looking to tap into as you make your way through the challenges of becoming the best cheerleader you can possibly be.

Accept the challenges—and face them with a positive attitude. Your goals will be that much more within reach.

Making eye contact with the audience or judges is a simple and effective way to maximize your cheerleading performance.

Don't worry about cheering well, just get up and cheer. When you do, cheer with passion. People won't care if you miss a step here or a word there, but if you cheer with more energy and enthusiasm than anyone else on the squad, you've gone a long way toward becoming a great cheerleader.

Your energy and enthusiasm can show through in many ways. For example, smiling and making eye contact is very important in cheerleading. They're two ways the cheerleader makes a connection with the fans in the stands or the judges at the competition. If you let your positive attitude shine through, your smiles and facial expressions will be genuine. The worst thing you can do with your expression is to look like you have a fake smile plastered on your face.

You want to make eye contact with your audience, too. Eye contact is a great way to communicate with those who are watching you. It tells them you're performing for them, not for someone else or, worst of all, just for yourself.

Who do you think has the more natural smile and eye contact, the cheerleader with the positive attitude or the one with the negative attitude?

A positive attitude will also help you keep your energy up. When your energy is up, you can better address some other important parts of cheerleading. For example, when you're in front of a crowd or a judge, and you're striking your poses and doing your chants and cheers, you want to be as crisp as possible in your movements. You don't want your audience to think you didn't get any sleep the night before. You also don't want to look like you don't have enough energy to get through the routine you're performing for your audience. That's an important point from dancing to keep in mind as a cheerleader. Consider the language: "the routine you're performing for your audience."

Generally, a dancer is someone who is performing for an audience. Sometimes, cheerleaders think they're just out there on the playing field to lend some support to the team, and that's about it. Nothing could be further from the truth. A cheerleader needs to think like a dancer, and

DO YOU HAVE THE RIGHT ATTITUDE?

Like dancers, cheerleaders take part in a very demanding physical activity. One false move, one wrong step, and the consequences could be serious. It could mean low marks from the judges, disqualification from a competition, or even an injury to one's self or another squad member.

Do you have the right attitude to be a cheerleader without messing things up for yourself or your squad? What follows isn't a fool-proof test of whether you have what it takes to be on a cheerleading squad or not, but it will give you an idea of the kinds of things that make for a positive attitude. For each statement below, answer yes or no.

- I hardly ever argue with my friends in anger.
- I maintain a high standard for myself where grades are concerned.
- People generally say I'm a positive person.
- My classmates look at me as someone who is willing to be helpful.
- My teachers generally have nice things to say about me.
- I'm not embarrassed to stand up in front of the classroom and speak.
- I think that having school spirit and loyalty is a good thing.
- I like to keep my appearance neat and clean.
- I value teamwork and welcome constructive criticism.

If you answered "yes" to six or more statements, you're well on your way to having the positive attitude of a great cheerleader!

Try to be as crisp as possible in every movement you make, even the simple ones.

that means thinking not just about doing cheers, but also about performing cheers. It also means thinking about the people in the stands not just as spectators at a game, but as an audience for your performance. Think like a dancer: when you go out there in front of a crowd, you're actually on stage in front of an audience.

As a cheerleader, you need to keep the right attitude off the field or the competition floor, too. You want to show everyone that you're serious about what you're

Whether you are dancing or cheering, you will need to have a lot of energy and enthusiasm.

doing. You want to demonstrate for your coach, the judges, and most of all for yourself, that you're there to do your best. That means that you need to do whatever it takes to show up on time for practices. If you have a serious attitude about your cheerleading, it means you practice at home in addition to practicing with the squad and your coach.

If you have dedication inside of you, that dedication will shine through. It will become clear to everyone that you're not just on the team for the sake of wearing the uniform.

In *A Dancer's World,* ballerina Margot Fonteyn wrote, "A dancer should be determined, receptive, patient, and possess a strong sense of self-awareness. He or she must be able to accept criticism readily, for this is a common element in a dancer's life. Above all, and it may seem obvious to state this, a dancer should love to dance."

Substitute the word "cheerleader" for "dancer" and Margot Fonteyn's words still ring true. In short, a cheerleader should be determined and patient, and above all should love to cheer.

Maintaining a proper and positive attitude is a skill. It can be learned, just like a cheer or a routine can be learned. It also needs to be practiced so that the skill isn't lost. Once learned, though, it's a skill that will serve you well as a cheerleader, and as a person, for the rest of your life.

Stretching

One of the most important things that a cheerleader can learn from a dancer is to prepare properly. The correct preparation for performance means that the dancer—or the cheerleader—will be able to perform at her best, while also avoiding unnecessary injuries.

Both dancing and cheerleading are very physical activities. To be a dancer or a cheerleader requires a wide range of body motions. Arms and legs are moving this way and that, bodies are jumping into the air, and without the proper preparation, injuries will occur.

The importance of proper stretching is something all cheerleaders must learn. Before any practice, before any

A proper warm-up is essential before you start cheerleading. You want to get the blood flowing through your body and warming up the muscles to avoid the risk of injury.

competition, before any cheerleading activity, you must remember to stretch your muscles.

"All dance classes start with warm-up exercises," wrote Cheryl Tobey in *Modern Dance.* "Stretching helps increase your range of motion and avoid injuries."

The same thing should apply to all cheerleading practices and performances. Start with the proper warm-up and stretching exercises. You'll feel better while cheering, and you'll be doing what needs to be done to avoid hurting yourself.

A typical warm-up routine actually takes place in three parts: warming up, limbering up, and stretching.

To warm up, you want to do about five minutes of light aerobics. This is a low-impact kind of exercise that helps raise your body temperature and prepare your muscles for the more demanding stretches to come. In low-impact aerobics, you aren't doing any high kicks or leaps, and you're keeping one foot on the ground at all times.

Examples of low-impact aerobics include marching in place or walking at a brisk pace. After about five minutes of this sort of physical activity, you're ready for limbering up.

"It is important to ensure that before going on to stretch the various muscle groups, the dancer gently mobilizes each of the joints through their full range of movement," says David Slade, a writer for the Web site CriticalDance.com. This technique is equally important for cheerleaders. Slade recommends the following movements which should be done after a warm-up and before actual stretching begins:

1. Turning, raising, lowering, and tilting the head.
2. Rolling the shoulders forward and back.
3. Circling the arms forward and back.
4. Flexing and extending the hands, wrists, and elbows.
5. Pointing and flexing the feet.
6. Flexing and extending the knees.
7. Circling the leg at the hip.

Here is some more in-depth discussion of the movements that can be done after warm-up and before actual stretching to help limber your body in preparation for stretching.

SHOULDER ROLLS

Roll both shoulders together in circles in both the forward and backward directions. This is effective not only in limbering up the shoulders, but also the base of the neck.

ARM CIRCLES

Extend your arms straight out to your sides, then make small circles in the air with your hands. Make clockwise circles for a count of 10 or 20, then reverse direction for another count of 10 or 20.

FLEXING AND EXTENDING

One at a time, flex and extend your hands, wrists, elbows, knees, and feet. This helps loosen your joints so that they can handle a full range of motion without becoming injured.

LEG CIRCLES

Lie on your back and make small circles with your entire leg, foot to hip. Your knee should be relaxed so that your hamstring muscle doesn't get in the way of your movements. Leg circles can also be done while lying on your side.

ALWAYS WORK WITH A COACH OR TRAINER

It's important to remember that when you engage in a very physical activity like cheerleading, you need to work with people who have more knowledge and experience than you do. They can help you learn, and they can help you avoid injuries.

Just as you wouldn't treat yourself medically without talking to a doctor, you should not start training yourself physically without talking to coaches or trainers.

The warm-up and stretching exercises in this chapter are techniques that are commonly used in dancing classes. They are often used by cheerleading squads, too. However, they are only examples. This should not be looked at as a recommended program to be followed regularly.

Cheerleading is becoming more and more physical all the time. The demands on cheerleaders are growing year after year.

A football team or a basketball team wouldn't take to the field or the court without proper coaching and physical training. Cheerleaders shouldn't start cheering without proper coaching and physical training, too.

The bottom line: work with your coach to develop a proper warm-up and stretching routine.

In order to be ready for the physical demands of cheerleading, it is important that your squad develop a stretching routine.

Once you've warmed up and limbered up under the watchful eye of your coach or trainer, you're ready for stretching.

According to Paul Blakey, author of *Stretching Without Pain,* the order in which different parts of the body are stretched is important. He suggests stretching the body in the following order for the best results.

Start with the upper and lower back, then stretch both sides. After that, stretch the arms, then stretch the chest. Move down to the buttocks and groin muscles, then the

Stretching after a practice is a great way to relax you and your muscles.

calves, then the hamstrings. Move on to the shins, then finish by stretching the quadriceps muscles.

The specific types of stretches you want to do will be determined by the specific types of routines you're doing. If your cheerleading routine includes splits, for example, then you will want to focus on leg stretches.

Many books and articles have been written on proper stretching technique. The number of actual stretching techniques used by dancers is equally large, and you could easily find hundreds of stretching exercises on the Internet or at your local library. Which ones are right for you? Only you and your coach or trainer, working together, can properly answer that question.

What follows are a few stretches commonly used by dancers. These are suitable for cheerleaders, too. They should give you an idea of the wide range of stretching exercises that can be done to prepare for cheerleading.

IMPORTANT: Do not try these stretches without proper physical preparation and the advice of a coach or trainer who can help you to stretch properly. Some of these stretches may not be able to be completed in their entirety unless you've been stretching and increasing your flexibility for many weeks or even months. Stretching techniques that are right for one person may be wrong for another person, so work with your coach or trainer to find the kinds of stretches that work best for you.

SIT-DOWN STRETCH

Sit on the ground with your legs extended out in front of you. Relax your hands by your sides without putting any weight on them, and point your toes slightly. Anchor yourself in place by tightening your buttock muscles; squeeze them gently together. Keeping your shoulders relaxed, imagine that there is a pole running straight up your spine. Then imagine yourself getting taller along the pole, sliding up it with your back as straight as it can be. Extend your neck and head along the imaginary pole, too.

STRAIGHT-LEGGED TOE-TOUCH

While standing, keep your legs straight, either together or spread shoulder width apart. Bend at the waist while you attempt to touch your toes or the floor. Be aware of your knees while performing this stretch, especially if you're doing this stretch with your legs apart, as you don't want to hyperextend them. Stretch gradually and slowly, and do not bounce. Be careful, because this position can place a great deal of pressure on your lower spine.

DOWNWARD DOG

In this stretch, a favorite of modern dancers, you make an upside-down V shape with your body. Your feet and hands are touching the floor as you're facing the floor, and you're bent at the waist. Your weight is on your hands and your feet. As you push the palms of your hands into the floor, the backs of your legs will be stretched.

QUADRICEPS STRETCH

While standing up, hold on to a stationary object like the edge of a wall or a bar with your right hand, so that you can maintain your balance. Bend your right knee, and bring your foot toward your buttocks. As you keep your left knee slightly bent, hold on to your right ankle with your left hand. Slowly pull your leg up and back, bringing your foot as high as comfortable. Do the same stretch with your left leg and your right hand.

SIDE TORSO STRETCH

Start by lying on your back with your arms extended to your sides and your knees bent with your feet flat on the floor. Bend your knees slowly to one side of your body while turning your head to the other side. Then bring your knees across to the other side of your body while turning your head in the opposite direction. You should feel the muscles stretching across your back.

CALF STRETCH

Start in a standing position. While keeping your right heel on the ground, take a large step forward with your left foot. Hold the position, then return to standing and repeat the stretch with your left heel on the ground, stepping forward with your right foot. Be sure to keep your body upright, your back straight, and your abdominal muscles tight.

DON'T OVERDO IT

Can you stretch too much? Yes. As Christine Dion wrote in the September 2000 issue of *Dance Spirit* magazine, "Dancers stretch endlessly. After all, dance technique requires excessive flexibility. But don't stretch too far— pushing your muscles beyond their normal range of motion can be harmful."

Cheerleaders should pay attention to that warning, too. When you stretch, you want to be careful not to over-stretch. The idea is to increase your body's flexibility without stretching so far that you cause damage to your muscles. That's why when you stretch, you need to do so slowly and gradually.

Stretching too far will cause what's called "microtrauma" to the muscles. That means the muscles experience very tiny tears, which may heal with scar tissue. When that happens, the muscle becomes less flexible, which is exactly the opposite of why you're stretching in the first place.

A hip hop dancer performs a jump similar to the toe touch jump used by cheerleaders. This kind of jump requires a lot of flexibility.

LEGS UP AND OVER

Start out by lying on the floor with your legs straight and your arms extended over your head. With your knees locked, lift your legs so they are at a 90-degree angle with the floor. Slowly extend your legs backward until they're parallel with the floor. Point your feet to the floor, and slowly lower your legs until your feet touch the floor.

It is very important to remember that you don't want to overstretch your body. Relax yourself mentally while you stretch, and move your body in a slow, gradual way so that you stretch your muscles without tearing them. Breathe slowly while stretching, and take longer to breathe out than you do to breathe in. Never bounce your body while stretching, and never hold a painful stretch.

Respect your body and listen to what it has to say. Pain is a warning signal. If you stretch properly, you should not be sore the day after stretching. If you're experiencing a problem, or noticing the beginnings of pain from your stretching, discuss it immediately with your coach or trainer.

Proper stretching is an important way to prepare your body for the physical demands of cheerleading. Many squads have a stretching routine they use that has been developed over time. Understand the importance of proper stretching, and don't scrimp on the time you spend warming up and stretching. Your body will thank you.

Choreography

In dance, "choreography" means the way movements are structured in order to form a dance. When music is involved, choreography also involves the art of synchronizing physical movements with appropriate music.

Physical movements can be drawn from any style of dance. They can also be brand-new movements that aren't popularly used in any dance style. The job of the choreographer is to create body movements that tell a story.

In the case of cheerleading, the story has to do with spirit. Cheerleading choreography should have the cheerleaders moving in ways that emphasize energy and

Whether you are dancing or cheering, your facial expression matters. Your expression not only shows your attitude, it helps to tell the story you are narrating through your choreography.

enthusiasm. Getting to that point, though, requires a lot of planning and hard work. For cheerleaders, it's the same kind of planning and hard work used every day by dancers.

When you watch a music video on television, you may say to yourself, "Wow, that looks so complicated! How do they learn to do all that?"

The way dancers learn complicated movements is by breaking a long dance down into small pieces.

"Take the choreography and break it down," explains Carol Lapidus Scott, an advisor for *Fit Magazine* and CEO of East Coast Alliance World Fitness Conventions. "Look at each eight-count and break down each move into its simplest form."

In other words, don't try to learn a whole dance all at once. Break it down into pieces, and learn it one piece at a time. Then put all the pieces together.

That's great advice for cheerleaders. Instead of trying to learn a whole cheer all at once, learn it a verse at a time. Instead of trying to learn the moves of a routine all at once, learn them one move at a time. Then put all the pieces together.

Andrea Kulberg, a writer for *Cheer Leader,* a magazine published by the British Cheerleading Association, explains what good choreography can mean to a cheerleading squad.

The squads that turn heads at stadiums, gymnasiums, and competition venues do more than the prerequisite of demonstrating a mastery of the skills of cheerleading. They

FAMOUS CHOREOGRAPHERS

While you may not know these artists by name, chances are you've probably seen their work on television, as they have worked on some of music's most famous videos. They are just a few of the most talented choreographers working today.

Darrin Henson

Darrin Henson has been called "choreographer to the stars" for his work with *NSYNC (their "Bye Bye Bye" video and several world tours), Britney Spears (her "Drive Me Crazy" video), Michael Jackson, Prince, Christina Aguilera (her "Genie In A Bottle" video), and Jennifer Lopez. He was voted Best Choreographer of the Year at the 2000 MTV Video Music Awards.

Tina Landon

A former Laker Girl cheerleader, Tina Landon won a 1999 MTV Video Music Award for Ricky Martin's "Livin' La Vida Loca," and received a "Best Choreography" MTV Video Music Award for Michael and Janet Jackson's "Scream." She also was nominated for a 1999 Emmy Award for Best Choreography for her work on Janet Jackson's "Velvet Rope" tour, which was broadcast on HBO. She's also choreographed music videos for Jennifer Lopez, including "If You Had My Love," "Waiting For Tonight," and "Feelin' So Good."

Fatima Robinson

Fatima Robinson has choreographed commercials for The Gap, worked on the movie *Save The Last Dance,* and developed choreography for such videos as Aaliyah's "Try Again," Will Smith's "Wild Wild West," Busta Rhymes' "Put Your Hands Where My Eyes Can See," the Backstreet Boys' "Larger Than Life," Santana's "Maria, Maria," and Brandy's "Baby."

Cheerleaders need to move in ways that emphasize enthusiasm. Even small moves, like the "elbows on the table" shown here, should be done with energy.

combine the athletic and graceful skills of cheerleading with a mastery of effective choreography.

How do you start learning effective choreography? How do you help your squad take its cheerleading to the next level? Step one is to know yourself and your teammates. In choreography, it's important to keep the skills of the cheerleading squad in mind. You don't want to attempt dance moves that are too complicated, or that the squad hasn't mastered yet. So step one to good choreography is making a list of what the squad is able to do. Don't set unrealistic goals, and don't attempt anything that's too complicated for your squad.

Step two is to choose your music. Of course, you want to pick music that's upbeat, energetic, and powerful. Once you've settled on the music you want to use for your routine, listen to it over and over and over again. Get to know every note and beat of the music. Once you do, you'll be able to break the music down into small pieces and start thinking about the types of moves that go with the sounds.

Step three is to match the moves of your squad to the sounds in the music. "The dance should tell a story," says Cindy Clough, author of *Just For Kix: A Collection of Advice, Inspiration, and the How To's of Running a Dance Team.* "It should have a definite beginning, middle, and end." Here are a few other tips Cindy provides for achieving good choreography:

- Don't try to do everything you know in one routine. Putting too many moves in will make the routine too busy.
- Make sure your routine has a strong beginning and a dynamite ending, but don't lose the middle of the routine.
- Make sure that movements flow. Have smooth transitions from move to move. You don't want it to look disjointed.

Try to think like a spectator. Imagine what the squad will look like to the crowd, or to the judges. Be creative! Be visual! If you're having fun in the routine, the spectators will have fun watching you. Be careful, though. Don't use a move in a routine just because it's fun to do. Make sure it fits into the total routine.

Finally, as a cheerleader, you owe it to yourself to do what a dancer does: practice, practice, practice. As you practice your choreography and start to put together all the pieces you learned separately, you will find that some of the pieces don't fit together so well. That's when it's time to change your choreography a bit. You may need to use an easier move here or a different move there.

These are the basics of choreography. Clearly, they can apply to cheerleading as well as dance. But how do you add more dance style into your basic cheerleading moves?

The answer to that question is simple. It boils down to a matter of personal taste. What sort of dance moves do you want to incorporate into your cheerleading? There's a whole wide world of dance styles. Each style has all kinds of variations within that style. And each variation has something from which cheerleaders can draw ideas and inspiration.

Lyrical dance, for example, includes elements of jazz dancing and ballet. In lyrical dance, the moves tell a story, and the moves flow from one to another very smoothly. The ease of flowing from move to move is good for cheerleading. A good cheerleading routine should flow from move to move without a lot of difficulty. The idea of

The easiest way to learn a new dance routine is to break it down into small pieces, then master each of the movements one at a time.

After each cheerleader has mastered the routine, the squad has to learn how to practice the moves in unison. Getting the proper synchronization takes time.

telling a story is one that cheerleaders can use, too. The softer nature of most lyrical dance, though, means that there aren't a lot of specific moves that will be good for cheering.

Jazz dance is closer in style to the types of dance you might see in many Broadway shows. Jazz dancing works well in big production numbers. Plays like *42nd Street* and *Fosse* incorporate impressive choreography that involves large groups of people. Michael Jackson's video for "Thriller" incorporated an energetic style of jazz-influenced group choreography. When you watch groups of people dancing in a coordinated way, you get more ideas of how to choreograph a group of cheerleaders.

Jazz dancing incorporates many moves seen in cheerleading. High kicks, jumps, and turns may be performed with gusto and energy in jazz dance. The same moves may be used in lyrical dance, too. The difference is that in lyrical dance, they'll often be performed with less speed and power, and with more grace and delicacy. The higher speed and more athletic nature of jazz dancing brings the spirit of the dance that much closer to the athleticism of cheerleading.

Hip hop may be the most diverse type of dance there is today. It's a very dynamic, athletic, and energetic style of dancing. It may also be the one style that will most influence cheerleading in the years to come. The dancing you see in music videos is likely to be a form of hip hop dancing. If it's not actually hip hop that you're seeing, it's probably been influenced by hip hop in one way or another. There are, it seems, an infinite range of skills and techniques included in hip hop dancing.

Locking, for example, is a hip hop technique in which the dancer locks into various positions. Locking was popularized in the 1970s by a musical group called The Lockers. Toni Basil, who had a hit song in 1982 called "Mickey," (which incorporated a cheerleading theme in its music video), was a member of The Lockers. Imagine a cheerleading squad working through a routine, locking into a synchronized position at the right moment in the music, then moving on. What a blend of dance and cheerleading that would be!

The dance technique called "contagion" is often used in hip hop. A movement is repeated from one person to the next. You've probably seen an example of contagion in hip hop when several dancers are holding hands in a line, and a dancer on one end does a rippling wave effect with his or her arms, and the wave is transferred from dancer to dancer on down the line.

Hip hop and cheerleading have a lot in common. Both are very athletic and energetic types of activities. That common energy makes hip hop a perfect place for cheerleaders to look for new moves and inspiration.

When most people think of choreography, they think of physical movements: the positions of the dancers or cheerleaders in relation to each other, the ways their arms and legs move, and the turns and jumps that make up the dance or cheerleading routine. But choreography is about facial expressions, too, and they can be just as difficult to master as the physical movements.

"Teaching real emotion is not easy," says Michelle Zeitlin, CEO of More Zap Productions and a choreographer for MTV music videos and TV commercials.

Many dancers adopt a certain look, either a "Disney" smile or pageant smiles or scowls. When I judge competitions, I see so many dancers, and you can pick what studio they come from. I try and get the dancers to connect to a real emotion that gets them excited and alive. So the face

It's important to choreograph your routine in such a way that each move flows easily and naturally into the one that follows it. Building these smooth transitions into your routine can make it look spectacular.

they express is not a "learned" face, but a real response to the movement and audience and music. Many times a cheerleader is so determined to be "sexy" that they end up looking coy instead of fresh and upbeat.

Practice your facial expressions in front of a mirror. It may feel strange at first, but it will help you have an expression that's natural, fresh, and upbeat.

A HERKIE BY ANY OTHER NAME

The language of dance wasn't created to describe cheerleading, but sometimes it seems that way. It's one of the many ways that dance and cheerleading are similar.

Take the *ciseauz,* for example. The ciseauz is a jump in which the dancer assumes the second position in the air, resembling a scissors. Second position in dance is when the feet are apart at slightly less than shoulder distance. Compare this move with the spread eagle in cheerleading. They're not exactly the same, of course, but they're quite similar. The spread eagle could almost be described as a high-energy, exaggerated ciseauz.

Maybe you have dance experience that allows you to do a switch leap. That's a move in which the dancer swings one leg forward then back, lifting the body into the air in a leap in which the legs are in a split position. It's not the same as a Herkie jump, but it's close, and it utilizes some of the same physical and athletic techniques.

Are you cheering *en haute?* Probably. In ballet, en haute refers to a position where the arms are above the head. The High V in cheerleading is an en haute move. What about a *grand jeté?* That's a big forward jump in dance. There are plenty of grand jetés in many cheerleading routines, too. Most likely, a good portion of those routines are taking place *par terre.* That's a dance term that means on the floor, as opposed to in the air.

Maybe you want to add a *pirouette* to your squad's routine. No, you don't have to wear frilly ballet tutus instead of cheerleading uniforms. Strictly speaking, a pirouette is a turn that's performed in place and on one foot. Get your squad to do that in unison to some funky music, and you have a sure crowd-pleaser.

Pay close attention to the language of dance. It probably describes cheerleading a lot more than you think.

In this chapter, we've touched on a few ways that dance choreography and styles can affect cheerleading techniques. The best way to learn about dance, though, is not to read about it, but to watch it and do it. Pay attention to the dance moves used in music videos and movies. Rent videos of Broadway plays that feature dancing. Talk to friends who know how to dance and ask them to show you new moves.

Dance is an enormous universe from which cheerleading can draw inspiration. It may seem too big sometimes, but don't let that discourage you. Developing a cheerleading routine is hard work. Choreography is also hard work. It's difficult for a single dancer to learn all the choreography necessary for a solo dance, but it's that much harder for a squad to learn all the pieces of a routine, put the pieces together, and perform them in proper synchronization.

The payoff, though, will be a cheerleading routine that wins cheers and awards. Good luck!

The Three F's

Dancers and cheerleaders have so much in common. They both have to think about the same kinds of issues. The Three F's—food, fitness, and fun—are three major issues both dancers and cheerleaders think about often.

FOOD

Maybe you've heard the phrase "garbage in, garbage out." It comes from the computer world. It means that if you feed a computer junk information, you'll get junk information sent back at you. The same theory applies to your eating. You have to eat healthy to be healthy. Take a

Without the proper nutrition, you won't have the energy to practice or perform your best in competition. It's especially important for cheerleaders and other athletes to eat plenty of healthy foods.

THE IMPORTANCE OF HEALTHY EATING HABITS

It goes without saying that as an athlete and a performer, you don't want to be loading up on junk foods. On the flip side of the coin, though, you don't want to become so obsessed with your body that you wind up ill because you're not eating properly.

Sadly, eating disorders affect as many as one in 10 young women. When people talk about eating disorders, they're usually talking about one of two things: anorexia nervosa or bulimia.

Someone who suffers from anorexia nervosa hardly ever eats. She is likely to be a perfectionist. She may also be a high achiever in school. At the same time, she suffers from low self-esteem. She thinks she's fat, even if everyone else agrees that she's thin.

Someone who suffers from bulimia will eat large amounts of food, then get rid of the food by forcing herself to vomit. Bulimics often use laxatives to rid their body of food as well.

Symptoms of eating disorders might include lots of complaints about feeling fat, a desire to over-exercise, questions about using laxatives, complaints of dizziness, and big changes in weight over a short period of time. Self-induced vomiting can also cause throat irritations and dental problems.

If you think you or a friend might be suffering from an eating disorder, talk to a parent, coach, or trainer immediately. Eating disorders are serious and they can lead to serious physical problems. In extreme cases, eating disorders can even be fatal.

Eat smart. Eat well. Be concerned about getting proper nutrition and eating the right foods, of course, but don't get obsessed about eating.

When you spend so much time with your fellow squad members, exercising together, practicing together, and performing together, you develop a special bond.

look at the food pyramid and see how it compares with your current eating habits. Remember that food is fuel for your body. If you put soda in a car's gas tank, it won't go anywhere. It's bad fuel for the car. The same thing is true of your body. Fill it with bad fuel, and you won't be able to go anywhere as a dancer or a cheerleader.

A lot of people don't know what they really eat in a day. They just eat. A good way to start paying attention to what you eat each day is to keep a food diary. Keep track of everything you eat every day, especially snacks. After a while, you'll begin to see where you can make smarter choices about the foods you eat.

Here are some good tips for smart eating:

- Avoid putting high-fat extras on your foods such as butter, mayonnaise, and salad dressings (try lemon juice instead).
- Eat slowly. It takes the body about 20 minutes to know it is full. If you eat slower, your body will be able to keep track of the food you're eating. In other words, you won't be giving your body more food than it really needs before it knows it already has it.
- Drink lots of water. Your body needs plenty of water each day. You'll also find that by drinking water, you won't snack on junk food as much.

Becoming obsessive about your eating is not the answer, either. The important thing is to eat in order to be healthy. Don't eat to lose weight. You need to maintain a proper weight for your particular body type. Don't set unrealistic and unhealthy goals for yourself—that's the first step toward becoming very unhealthy.

FITNESS

Fitness doesn't have to mean exercising like crazy. Some people hear the word "fitness" and they think it means joining a gym and going there to work out on weight machines for two or three hours every day.

Fitness simply means staying physically active. Of course, if you're interested in cheerleading, you probably are an active person already. Maybe you play sports.

Maybe you like jogging. Maybe you like running around the neighborhood playing with your friends. Maybe you like riding your bike, or you like to go swimming or rollerblading. All of these things, even walking, can contribute to a person's physical fitness.

As with proper eating, it's important to remember that you don't have to go to the extreme with proper fitness. Everybody likes to sit around and watch television sometimes. If your daily exercise amounts to getting up to find

WHAT'S A CALORIE?

Everyone always talks about calories. "This food has 450 calories," or "That activity burns 200 calories." Exactly what is a calorie?

A calorie is a measure of energy. A calorie is the amount of energy, or heat, it takes to raise the temperature of one gram of water one degree Celsius, or 1.8 degrees Fahrenheit.

The calories talked about with food or exercise are actually kilocalories. One kilocalorie is equal to 1,000 calories. So when someone says, "This candy bar contains 200 calories," that really means 200,000 calories.

An extra pound of fat in your body is equal to 3,500 calories. Fat is your body's way of storing energy. When you exercise, you're burning calories. When you burn calories, your body uses up fat. The amount of calories burned when you exercise depends on your weight. For the average young person, running will burn about 10 calories a minute, bicycling will burn about five calories a minute, and sitting quietly and watching television will burn about one calorie per minute.

The average person eats about 2,000 calories a day.

Cheerleading is hard work, but it's supposed to be fun, too, so don't forget to enjoy yourself and have fun with the other squad members while you work together to be a great team.

the remote control, though, then you ought to think about being a little more physically active.

According to Judy Young, the executive director of the National Association for Sports and Physical Education in Reston, Virginia, kids need a good amount of exercise. She says that school-age children between five and 12 years old should have at least one hour of moderate and/or rigorous activity every day. That activity is in addition to any physical education programs there might be in school. Moderate activity includes bike riding and general outdoor play. Rigorous activity includes running races and longer bike rides.

FUN

It sounds simple: have fun! Unfortunately, for some cheerleaders, it's too easy to forget to have fun. There are competitions, moves to learn, and practices to attend. It's a demanding schedule. You may want to go to the movies, but you can't because you have cheerleading practice again. On top of all that, there are worries about uniforms and makeup. Some kids may think cheerleading is stupid and tease you because you are a cheerleader. Don't listen to them.

Sure, there's a lot to remember about being a cheerleader. Don't get caught up in the worries, though. That's why you have coaches and trainers and parents.

Let your coach worry about whether you're doing the moves exactly right. Let your trainer worry about developing the proper routine for stretching before cheering.

Cheerleading is about having fun. After all, if you're not having fun, what's the point of all the hard work? You're a cheerleader. Congratulations! Enjoy it. You've earned it.

Glossary

arch – A position in which the back is curved.

chant – A short, repetitive yell performed continually throughout a game (example: "De-fense! De-fense!"), or a short routine with words sometimes involving the crowd.

cheer – A longer, more spirited yell that is performed only during official breaks of a game. Often, a cheer will utilize a variety of motions and stunts.

choreography – The way movements are structured in order to form a dance. Also, the art of synchronizing physical movements with appropriate music.

ciseauz – A dancer's jump in which the legs open in a second position in the air, resembling a scissors.

contagion (ripple) – The repetition of a movement from one person to the next.

en haute – In ballet, a position of the arms above the head.

glissade – In ballet, a gliding step which usually connects two steps.

grande jeté – A large leap forward.

handspring – A spring from a standing position to the hands, and back to a standing position.

Herkie – Also called the side hurdler. A type of jump in which one leg is straight and the other leg is bent. Named after Lawrence Herkimer, who started the first cheerleading company and ran the first cheerleading camp in the 1940s.

jump – A spring into the air in which both feet leave the ground and the body assumes a given position.

locking – A hip hop dance technique in which the dancer locks into positions.

lunge – A leg movement in which the feet are set wide apart, then the person moves in one direction, bending one leg so that the other leg is as straight as possible. The knee of the bent leg should be directly over that leg's ankle.

microtrauma – An injury to a muscle that occurs from overstretching.

par terre – In dance, steps performed on the floor as opposed to in the air.

pike – A position in which the body is bent at the hips and the legs are positioned straight out in 90-degree angles.

pirouette – A turn, performed in place and on one foot.

routine – A choreographed sequence of moves.

split – A position in which the legs are spread apart in alignment or sideways one in front of the other.

spotting – In dance, the fixing of the eyes on one spot as long as possible during turns to avoid dizziness and to keep one's orientation.

spread eagle – A type of jump in which the arms and legs are spread out to form a giant letter "X."

stag – A leap or pose in which one leg is bent and the other is straight.

straddle – A position where the legs are straight out and apart.

stunt – Any maneuver that includes tumbling, mounting, a pyramid, or a toss.

switch leap – In dance, to swing one leg forward then back, lifting the dancer into the air in a leap in which the legs are in a split position.

transition – A choreographed maneuver that enables a team to move from one highlighted stunt to the next.

Internet Resources

http://www.aacca.org/aacca/guidelines.htm

Cheerleading safety guidelines prepared by the American Association of Cheerleading Coaches and Advisers. Two sets of guidelines are provided: one for the high school level, and one for the college level.

http://www.americancheerleader.com

The official Web site of *American Cheerleader* magazine features message boards, chat, and a wide variety of articles available to subscribers.

http://www.cheerhome.com

This site calls itself "The home for cheerleading on the Web." Created in 1999 "for the benefit of cheerleaders and cheerleading coaches," CheerHome.com features news, message boards, articles, and plenty of resources for learning more about cheerleading camps, competitions, and college programs.

http://cheerleading.about.com/index.htm

An About.com directory of hundreds of Web sites, categorized by subject matters like Cheerleading 101, Cheers and Chants, Fundraising, Photo Gallery, and more. Specialized links like "Find A Competition Near You" are helpful. All this information is not just random search engine results, it's all organized by a personal About.com guide.

http://www.cheerleading.net

Cheerleading.net has links to hundreds of Web sites for cheerleaders and coaches at all levels. There are also categories for international cheering sites, cheer gyms, fundraising ideas, and more.

http://www.cheerleading.org.uk

The Web site of the British Cheerleading Association has information about championships, camps, and clinics in the United Kingdom. It also includes the online version of *Cheer Leader,* the journal of the British Cheerleading Association. It has hundreds of pages of articles which will be of interest to you no matter where you live.

http://www.dance.net

Dance.net provides an extensive selection of dance-related message boards, including ballet, tap, hip hop, jazz, and more.

http://www.dancemagazine.com

The official Web site of *Dance Magazine* includes articles and information about dancers and choreographers, news and reviews from around the world, and coverage of dance education.

http://www.nationalspirit.com/home.asp

The official Web site of the National Spirit Group, the parent company of the National Cheerleaders Association and the National Dance Alliance. The NCA was the group begun in 1948 by Lawrence Herkimer, who also organized the first cheerleading camp in 1949.

http://www.uca.com

The official Web site of the Universal Cheerleaders Association, a leader in cheerleading safety and stunt innovation, and one of the largest cheerleading camp providers and competition sponsors in the world.

http://www.varsity.com

A large amount of information and resources on both cheerleading and dance, Varsity.com is presented by Varsity Spirit, a leading supplier of cheering and dancing fashions and uniforms.

Further Reading

Chappell, Linda Rae. *Coaching Cheerleading Successfully.* Champaign, Illinois: Human Kinetics, 1997.

Clough, Cindy. *Just For Kix: A Collection of Advice, Inspiration, and the How To's of Running A Dance Team.* Brainerd, Minnesota: Just for Kix, 2000.

Fonteyn, Margot. *A Dancer's World: An Introduction for Parents and Students.* New York: Alfred A. Knopf, 1979.

French, Stephanie Breaux. *The Cheerleading Book.* Chicago: Contemporary Books, 1995.

Giordano, Gus. *Jazz Dance Class.* Pennington, New Jersey: Princeton Book Company, 1992.

Kuch, K.D. *The Cheerleaders Almanac.* New York: Random House, 1996.

Neil, Randy, and Elaine Hart. *The Official Cheerleader's Handbook.* New York: Fireside Books, 1986.

Rusconi, Ellen. *Cheerleading.* Danbury, Connecticut: Children's Press, 2001.

Scott, Kieran. *Ultimate Cheerleading.* New York: Scholastic, Inc., 1998.

Tobey, Cheryl. *Modern Dance.* Danbury, Connecticut: Children's Press, 2001.

Index

CRAIG PETERS has been writing about various aspects of sports and popular culture for more than two decades. His daughter, Alexandra, began her dance and cheerleading training when she was two years old. By the age of 13, Alexandra had competed on several school and recreation teams and been named captain of her middle school cheerleading squad. Craig has long ago given up the idea that this might be a passing fad for his daughter.